Once there was a kid named Lenny who lived in a mansion. He had been the first person to give people the idea of a time machine. There were lots of time machines after the kid came up with the idea. The time machine could also break and creatures would be coming randomly. The kid was a genius, so he figured out how to stop this. He needed lots of materials to stop it. He used string to cover up the broken part. Even the smallest tear could be bad. The time machines have been around for a long time and it is very rare for one to break. Time machines were tested and then sold to people for lots of money. The kid received lots of money. The people he worked with were informed and then made new inventions. The kid was sent to a school where he would learn how to create things. The boy was not like any other kid who went to a regular school. He had to figure out how to stop bigger problems with any machine. He has many friends who are smart.

The ordinary world of the story is the house the kid lives at. His parents were on a business trip, so he was alone with the butler. He recently bought a time machine and put it in his backyard. He had been studying more about different creations. His newest idea is to build robots based on animals that would help people. He had many animals to use and decided to use a time machine to find extinct ones. Although the kid lacked something, he was not able to focus when something distracted him. He is distracted easily. He needed to figure out how to have even more focus. He tried working everywhere in his house and outside. He decided to find animal toys at the store which might help him not be distracted. The animals could help because every time he is distracted, he could see the animal and remember not to be distracted. The boy tried this and it worked. He was able to study more and now finish with more time for other things like video games. Although he does not like to play video games much, he thinks it will help him have fun but also study about machines. The boy has been learning more and more about machines at his school, and he decided to build his own. He made his time machine, but they would not work. He started to get good news from the people who invented time machines. These people's company is the Time Workers. They have this big building where they come up with ideas and this factory where they build the time machines. The kid went to the factory, and thought it looked amazing. The factory had lights everywhere, which is what the kid liked the most. The lights were because of the Time Workers building their time machines. The kid saw a big place where they kept some animals like the dodo bird. The kid had some ideas, so he went to the building where the Time Workers come up with ideas. The Time Workers liked them, so they decided to use them. Each time machine should be different. An example would be that there should be a time machine that goes back to when Earth started, and the other goes even farther. The more back in time a machine goes, the more money it costs. The time machines that traveled less back in time were smaller. They all would start small, and there is a button that would make it fold out and let you travel through time. Many people have already traveled through time. The kid went back to his house and his butler said he traveled through time. He said it was amazing. The time machine the boy owned could travel to when Earth is created. The kid played his new video game and then slept after he ate his dinner. The next day, he went to the machine school, which was Tech Academy, and learned about how time machines worked. He knew this already, because the idea of time machines came from him. People from Time Workers came and gave each person

materials to create a model of a time machine. These time machines wouldn't work at all,

because there are no wires, buttons, batteries, or gears. After Tech Academy, the boy went to his

house, which is a mansion, and the he ate his lunch, which was a sandwich.

The call to adventure is when the kid does some research and then looks at his toy. The toy

reminded him to time travel and take pictures of extinct animals. He then took a camera for

pictures and food in case he stayed there for some time. The kid forgot about Tech Academy, so

he went there to tell them where he is traveling. He also went to Time Workers and told them he

is finally going to travel through time. The Time Workers had been coming up with new ideas

when he came. The boy then went to his mansion to time travel. The kid researched some more

before going. Then he wanted to travel. The butler had given him a note about researching, so he

went and researched even more. He gets called to the travel by the butler, who wants to travel

with him. The boy travels and then finds a note. The kids best friend came over the other day to

travel, and then the machine broke. The kid then came inside to find out what he needed to fix

the time machine. He found the tools and fixed it. Then he found out the real adventure for him.

He found out the real adventure is to create robotic dinosaurs that would help people, and the

only way to do it is to find dinosaur bones. He went to a museum and took pictures. The dinosaur

bones are so large, especially the plant eaters. Then he went to the zoo and took pictures. The

butler told him to find the biggest dinosaur bone. He found out that his adventure would need the

biggest dinosaur bone. The boy searched and searched, then, finally he found it. The world's

largest dinosaur bone. It is bigger than any building, just the bone. The kid needed to figure out how to take it to his house. The kid brought it back and then found his friend playing sports. The kid wanted to play too, so he went. There the kid finds out that he has not played sports much.

The kid goes back to his house and then realizes that he does not want to travel. He thought about it, and then he decided not to. He wanted to make sure traveling was safe, so he asked the Tech Academy. They said it was safe and many people have done it. He knew it was safe, he wasn't sure if the time machine would break. Tech Academy said it would not break. The kid returns home and receives a letter from his best friend saying he wants to travel. The mansion with the bone came into his mind. Traveling could help figure out which dinosaur bone it was. The genius decided not to. He thought it was too dangerous. (This is how he refuses the adventure.) The genius went to his house after telling his friend no. The genius started playing video games to stop thinking about traveling. He then went to hid computer to research. The genius looked up dinosaurs to see how big each one is. Some dinosaurs were so much smaller than the bone. Then he went to the store and bought more toys. He would observe the toys then the bone. He could not figure out which dinosaur it belonged to. Then he researched every toy. The genius had to figure out who the bone belonged to. The butler came and told him his parents are coming. The genius was happy and asked when. The butler said in a few days. The genius kept on researching for the dinosaur. He took it to the museum and they said they knew dinosaurs, but not this one. The museum offered to display it. The kid gave it to be displayed. He received lots of money for it. The kid knew he discovered this new species. He thought paleontologists could help, so he went there. They are experts, and they don't know it. The genius offered to name it, and the paleontologists said yes. The genius needed to find some name for this dinosaur. He went to his house and asked the butler. The butler couldn't think of any, either. Then the kid thought if he could see this dinosaur. He still would not time travel, though. So he decided to name it by looking for more bones. He told the paleontologists and they found the skull. It was definitely a plant eater, so he has a visual aid. He thought the name should be plantosaur, which meant plant lizard. The genius could not believe he found the biggest dinosaur. The plantosaur was placed at the museum after all the bones were found. The plantosaur was over 300 feet tall, so the museum put it outside. The bones were very heavy, and trucks could barely move with the bones. The genius viewed the display and thought it was so amazing. Lots of people came to see the plantosaur, and people wanted to travel through time to see it. That reminded the kid, he still would not time travel. The kid decided to go to Tech Academy to learn more. The genius told his friends about the dinosaur. His friends were impressed. They made cake for the event. It was dinosaur shaped and was chocolate, the genius's favorite. The friends ate the cake and then they talked about traveling. They asked if the genius was ready yet, and he said he was not. He said they could come to his house and use the time machine. The friends came to his house and traveled. The friends asked one more time, then traveled. When they came back, they said it was awesome. They said they noticed the plantosaur. The genius then knew he wants to go. But he kept thinking about the machine breaking when he would want to travel.

The genius meets his mentor at the Time Workers. His mentor was not working there, just someone who wanted to go on an adventure. He does not work there, but he met the kid and heard the adventure. His mentor became a mentor when they met and then the genius knew he is a very smart person. The mentor knew about the past, because he has traveled there lots of times.

He knows lots of dinosaurs, and is ready to help. The genius decided that this guy was an expert, so he asked if he could be a mentor. The mentor said yes, and then they went to the genius's house to see the time machine. The mentor knew what to do when the time machine breaks while you are in the future or past. The mentor knew the time machine is not breakable. Even if it is grabbed by a T rex, it will not break. The genius knew this is safe, so he went. When they arrived at the dinosaur time, there were lots of dinosaurs. The two people found an empty area full of dinosaurs, so they went behind some bushes. The mentor talked to the genius about the dinosaurs. The mentor said he knew where lots of plantosaurs are. The plantosaurs are so large, they are five hundred times the size of a blue whale. This means the genius found the young plantosaur, which is a hundred times bigger. The genius followed the mentor until they found the plantosaur forest, as the mentor said. The mentor then noticed some large dinosaur. Of course, it was a T rex, which looked microscopic to a plantosaur. The plantosaur turned its head and grabbed the T rex. It then threw it across the forest. The genius and mentor knew they should not be near the plantosaur. The the plantosaur noticed them. They ran to another forest, where they decided they should bring the time machine. They went back, only to find it went somewhere. Now they were trapped. This is why the boy never time traveled. He could never get the right calculations about if the time machine would stay or not. They now built a house out of trees.

The next day, the two people had finished their house without sweating. This is because they built it slowly. The water supply is almost out, so the genius went to the river. Then he found something about his size. Then the genius ran back to the house. He knew what it is. The genius gave the water supply to the mentor and told him about what had happened. The mentor knew how to avoid these dinosaurs. He said do not run, because they will run, too. He said to stand still, so it does not run. The mentor then knew the dinosaur came. They went inside. Then the dinosaur scratched the wood. The velociraptor cut through a log of wood. The two stood still like statues. The velociraptor thought they are statues, so it left. The two people built a stronger house. Then something scratches part of the roof. It crashes its head inside. The house fell and they are trapped. The T rex leaves after not seeing anyone. The two people are not crushed, they jumped right in time and then did not move. They decided to not build wooden houses. They had to make sure they would not just glue wood together, so they worked hard on it. Then the house had been glued together with glue and mud. The wood is made stronger, and they made it look like the background of trees by painting it. The house would not be noticed by dinosaurs, only by them. The mentor had been walking outside when all of a sudden something zooms past him. The genius came outside to see, and it was a velociraptor. The velociraptor ran past the mentor before he then took him to the forest. The kid needed to help the mentor, but he needs something. He looked through the supplies and found something that would help. He found the velociraptor so he threw the can of meat at it. The velociraptor looked at the genius, then the can. It took the can and ran away. The genius then only found the mentors hat and note. He wrote a note about everything about dinosaurs. The genius realized what happened to the mentor. The genius is now trapped. Now he would not know how to escape. The genius went to his house to think. What dinosaur could have stolen the time machine, then the thought it was the T rex. The genius remembers seeing something metal in the T rex's mouth. The problem is that it is a T rex. The genius took more meat, he had tons of food. The T rex then spit something and ran away. The genius thought it would not be this easy. He too the machine and went back. He went to when he talked to the mentor. He told him what would happen. The mentor then stayed. The kid returned to his own time, and the mentor is still his friend. The mentor will not remember what happens at the dinosaur time, because he never went. The kid took a hammer, and smashed his machine.

The butler told the genius that his parents are visiting South America. The genius knew his parents are now close to where he is. The genius went to the backyard and found an egg the size of the genius. He picked up the egg and saw it hatch. The egg hatched into a plantosaur. The boy is amazed. He then looked at the machine. He opened the door and noticed the lights. The boy knew what each color is. The different time periods. The genius went inside and the butler said there is a baby triceratops at his room. The boy went to see and the triceratops was there at his room. The genius told the butler what happened and the boy went to Time Company and then talked to them about the machine. Time Company stopped selling machines till they found out how to fix them. The genius asked Tech Academy and they still needed to research. It is a lesson later. The genius went to his house to try and figure it out himself. He could not figure it out either. Then a panther walked to him. The boy stood still and treated the panther as if it were a pet. The panther became happy and did not attack anyone. The boy thought the panther is his pet, so he left it outside. Obviously the butler or his parents would not want a panther in the house. The boy knew if the butler treated the panther meanly, the panther would be mean. The genius knew the panther would make sounds. The butler may be suspicous, so he said it is the neighbors cat looking at the machine that is broken. The genius went to feed the panther some food, he just fed it cat food. After all, he is a cat. The genius knew more creatures came. There were more eggs that the boy found near his trees. The backyard was huge, so creatures could be everywhere, especially because there are lots of trees. The genius came back with a bowl of crumbs and the butler noticed the bowl. The butler said the cat is the neighbors, so they feed it. The genius said the cat needed some energy to climb the wall, so he fed him. The butler asked if the machine is better, and the genius said not yet. Now the genius had to deal with a panther, and the creatures.

The special world is when the boy finds out the animals are coming from the time machine. The special world is at his ordinary world. The boy now needs to figure out how to stop the machine. The enemy comes when the time machine combined two things. Someone coming from a time machine, and some kind of panther. The panther is evil and the boy tries to be nice. The panther is evil as the panther said and he said he is the one who is causing the creatures. The panther will not tell the boy how to stop this, so he needs to figure it out. The panther tries to bring more animals by using magic. The magic was purple andbrought more animals. There would be different animals from different times and some animals combined together. the butler found the boy and took him outside. The mansion then glowed purple and the panther came on top to talk to the boy. The panther had now brought more animals and the boy could not stop it. The panther made sure the boy would not use any magic to stop it. The boy went inside and then to the backyard to take the machine. The panther tried to stop him but it was too late. The boy ran outside and then ran more. The panther tried magic to stop the boy, but it didn't work. The panther then used magic to release animals, but it didn't work. The boy had been blocking it. The boy stopped to make sure the panther stopped. The panther stayed at the mansion. The neighborhood came outside to see what was happening. The boy went to the mentor to ask him what was happening. The mentor told the boy how to stop this. The mentor helped the boy for a while until a creature took him. It was a tiger. The boy looked outside and saw the panther. The boy's pet panther was fighting the evil panther. The evil panther used magic to make the panther evil but it didn't work. The panther ran after the boy. The boy caught some magic and used it for the panther. The panther now helped the boy. The boy sent the panther to the machine. The boy ran and the panther came back and kept sending animals. The boy used magic to make the animals help him. The boy had lots of animals on his side, but the panther had more. The boy went to his house and the went inside. There was a note from his mentor. The mentor cleared the house and the tiger. The mentor had went to the panther. The mentor knew how to stop this and left a note which told the boy about how to stop it. The boy went outside and then he found his machine was not there. There are still lots of pieces of magic dust. There was a jar of purple magic and the boy used it. He could now help stop the panther. The boy looked for the panther, who is being fought by the mentor. The boy gave the mentor some more magic, and the mentor used it. The panther was weakened for about an hour. The boy and mentor worked on the machine that would stop the panther. The boy had lots of materials and the exact ones. The mentor put it together and the boy tested it on some cardboard. The machine would return the panther back to normal. The boy and mentor finished in two hours. The panther came tired. he wanted to sleep, so he fell on the couch. The two tried to use the machine but it didn't work. The boy and mentor didn't know why. the boy then knew about the panther's forcefield. The pet panther came from the backyard and pulled the forcefield from the panther. The panther then used the forcefield. The boy then used the machine and the panther could not use magic. The panther could not become human again, but now he is less powerful. The mentor trapped the panther in a cage and then took the cage with them. He wrapped some layers of locks around the panther. The panther woke up later. The boy and mentor didn't know what to do with him. The panther had not been evil anymore. Surprisingly, the panther now had been nice. The magic turned him evil. The panther said he wants to live at a house. The mentor and boy built a house that was strong for the panther. The panther told them he would not be evil. The mentor then unlocked the cage for the panther and the panther lived at the house. The panther had been happy and then found this magic jar. He opened it and then started using magic to help. (Special Place)

The panther kept using magic and then became evil. The boy went to see the panther before he became evil and the panther had been watching television. The boy and the panther talked for some time and then the boy left. The boy started seeing some magic around the panther's house. The boy knew the panther became evil again. The panther could fly with the magic and he brought animals from the machine. The boy found his pet panther because he wanted to tell him to fight the evil panther. The panther could not be controlled by evil magic, only good magic. The panther went to the time machine and broke it. Everything went back to normal and the panther lost his magic. The panther was still evil. The boy knew the time machine would not work. The panther could not send any more animals from the machine. The panther made his house bigger and moved somewhere else. The boy went to the panthers house to see if the panther had become good or not. The panther was still evil and trapped the boy. The boy had to find out how to make the panther good. The time machine would still send out creatures. The panther fixed it and then the boy needed more plans. The panther made sure the machine is now fixed and that it would not break. The panther talked to to boy and then released him. The boy pretended to be on the panther's side and helped him. The panther then took the boy to his house and the boy had the perfect plan. The next day, he went to the panther and then the panther knew he was not really evil. The panther could tell by the way the boy talked he was not evil. The boy then needed to have some new plan. The boy thought about some plans but needed more time. The panther came and then told him to build an evil machine. The boy said he would do it if the panther would not be super evil. The panther agreed and the boy built a machine that would help instead of sending more animals. The panther let the boy go to his mansion and then the boy thought more. All of his plans could not work. Then he thought about taking the machine. He took his time machine from the panther while he was busy. The boy then used it to go to when the panther found the magic at his house. The boy took the magic then let the panther live there. The boy went back to his own time and everything was fixed. The panther was not evil and the boy still had to deal with animals coming out. The boy needed to ask the panther if he knew how to stop the animals from coming. The panther needed magic to remember, and the boy knew he would not give the panther magic. The panther now could not help. The boy had to figure this out on his own. The boy needed to first fix the time machine. The time machine still had the marks from when the boy smashed it. The boy built robots that might help out with this problem. He used magic to give them the knowledge they need to help out. The boy knew the robots help out because he programmed them. He has built robots before, and none have become evil. He fixed the time machine and then the machine was fixed. The panther had been in his house and the boy told him what happened. The panther wanted to be friends with the boy. The panther that was once his enemy is now his friend. The panther came to his house to see it. The pet panther also liked this panther as a friend. The boy showed the panther his house and then the butler noticed the big panther. The butler asked what was happening, and the boy needed to explain.

The boy told the butler what had been happening and that it was the panther not the neighbor's cat the whole time. The butler told him that his parents are coming soon and they would not want to have a pet panther. The panther said he is a friend and he will help out with what the boy or butler needs. The panther went back to his house. The boy went to his house and found the boy at the mansion. The boy said he just saw the panther at his house. Then the panther took the boy to his house. The panther was good and just wanted to show the boy how he was doing. The panther then noticed the time machine disappeared. The time machine had just disappeared there. The boy was now stuck at the future unless there was a time machine he can buy. (Special Place)

The panther was lying. He was always evil. The boy figured it out a few days later. The boy visited the panther and the panther trapped him. The panther had been working hard on a new machine. He used magic to make his house a mansion. The boy escaped and left the panther. The boy went to his house and the time machine was glowing with a bright light. The boy went to see what was happening, and he saw that there were too many animals coming. The time machine eventually exploded and there were animals at the boy's backyard. The boy needed to find out how to stop this so he tried to fix the time machine. He fixed it, but it didn't help. The boy knew his plans always failed. The boy didn't have any plans. Then he just went inside to work. He knew he was great at fixing things and calculating things, but he could not figure this out. He knew his mansion was now surrounded by animals. At his backyard, animals, at his front door, the panther. He was stuck at his mansion. The panther used his claws to try to get into the mansion. The animals broke some of the backyard door. The boy had to find out how to make things go back to normal. He went outside to the panther and the panther tried to take him to his mansion but the boy ran past him. The boy ran and then threw a trash can at the panther's house. The panther liked how it looked and then was distracted. The boy ran to the back door of the panther's mansion and went inside to steal the machine. The machine would help him a lot. The boy took the machine and it captured the panther in a glass box. The panther was shrunk and the boy left the panther in his mansion. The panther could not escape his own invention. The boy then took the glass box off and sealed it and poked air holes at it. The boy took the machine and captured all the animals. The boy took the bigger glass box off and sealed it then sent them back to where they came from after opening the box at the machine. The boy visited the panther who escaped from the glass box. He built the machine again with magic and trapped the boy. He sealed the box to make sure it was not breakable. The boy tried to escape and knew it is possible to escape. He escaped and then created inventions to help him. The panther took the inventions after coming to the boys house and used them for his big machine. The boy took the machine and took a hammer and smashed it. The panther went to the boys house then took the boy to then put him in a small box where the only way to escape is when the panther says that he can. The boy made his voice sound like the panther so he could escape the boy took the panthers machine and made it into a helmet that could make the panther do what he wants. The boy went to the panthers house and then used the machine to make the panther good. Lenny took his brick system toys and he made something that looked like the panther. He thought it was great, so he went to the panthers house and showed him. The panther wanted it, but the boy kept it. Lenny took the toy to his house and the panther came every day for it. Lenny eventually gave it to him, but it was not the real one. Once the panther put it down, it would not move. It was stuck to the table and the panther could not get it off. The panther did not mind. Then someone came over to buy the table from him, and he wanted it to be empty. Now the panther needed to find out how to take the toy off of the table and put it somewhere else. The boy went to his backyard and there were lots of animals coming out of the portal again, and this time they were made out of clay. Now the boy lived in a stop motion world, and the animals teeth just felt soft. The boy knew this would not be bad. There was a T rex that tried to bite him but it didn't work. The dinosaurs teeth became small and crushed. The dinosaur tried to stomp on a rock, but the rock stuck on his foot. The time machine was now made out of clay, too. The panther came by, made out of bricks. The panther used magic to make everything like this. The boy tried not to tell the panther about how awesome this was. The boy looked at what he used to fix the machine, and what he used would turn things that went through clay or back to normal. The boy went inside and then played games

The boy went through the time machine and then when he arrived where he wanted to be, he was clay. The boy was now able to do lots of things. The boy went to Rome in ancient times and then people noticed him. They knew he was clay, and they were surprised. They treated the boy nicely and gave him what he wanted. Then there was a flash of light where the boy came and then something came. The panther came and he was made out of clay. The boy talked to him and then he threw a rock at his arm. The panther's arm fell off and the boy threw more rocks. The panther started throwing rocks too, but the clay would grow back quickly. The boy asked the panther where the time machine was, and the panther said it goes back to the boy's house. The boy was stuck at Rome with his arch enemy in ancient times. The boy fought the panther, but he knew it would not help. The boy was stuck clay for a long time now. The boy needed something to help him. The panther was still enemies with the boy and he purposely made the time machine disappear. The boy could not fix it, because whatever he had was made out of clay. Even his food, which is edible when you are clay. Clay food actually tasted normal and the panther thought so too. The boy took his tools to build himself a house. The boy set up televisions, and they worked. The boy then thought he could build himself a time machine. He got to work and then when he was tired, he slept. He liked Rome, but he wanted to get back to his home. The boy was treated well because he looked magical. He looked like stop motion, which he was. The boy went to see the panther, and he had been working like the boy. The panther had actually been nice and then asked if they could team up to get back home. The boy was so surprised, but he thought the panther was just tricking him. The panther had more clay than the boy, and the panther was more experienced with machines. The panther said he was not tricking the boy at all and that he was serious about helping him. The boy invited the panther to his house and they worked on the time machine. The boy was also really smart, he could build machines and do lots of algebra. He could tell if the time machine was good or not. Also, if it is safe. The clay machine he was building would allow anyone who is clay to return to normal, or someone to become clay. When the boy tested it out, it would not work. It just made lights. The panther's machine was just like the boy's. They seemed the same, except they had different lights. The boy and panther became friends and the panther said he knew how to find the most important piece for a machine. The panther had been to Rome because when he was human, he was from Rome. The panther said the place had been there for a very long time, so it is probably there. The place was really amazing, it must have been brought from the future. The panther said it was built in ancient times and finished later on. The panther's friend brought it, and the panther's friend was there. There were cars here, even Ferrari's. The boy was surprised someone could place this at a machine. The boy had gotten lots of respect in Rome, so he got a toy version of a Ferrari. The panther got the

piece and used it for the machines. They still would not work. The boy knew he had to figure out

how to make the machine work. The boy gave up and threw rocks at the machine. The rocks

stuck at the machine. The panther said that he should not have smashed it. The panther was very

smart, one of the things that he had not known about the panther. The boy thought his butler

would be wondering where he was, and when he sees the pet panther and the clay animals, he

will be surprised. The butler in fact noticed the animals but was happy. The boy knew the butler

would be happy but would still not want the animals. The boy and panther started becoming

good friends, and the panther was no longer evil. He had green eyes, which mean he is nice.

When they are purple, he is evil. The boy liked the panther better. (The Innermost Cave). The

people of Rome kept treating the boy and panther respectfully. If the boy asked for something,

the people would get it for him or the panther. The panther had not thought about ever being evil.

The boy heard him say this, so he was very happy. The Romans had been building lots of

buildings like the Colosseum. The boy had went to these buildings and some were made of clay.

The boy found some statues out of colorful clay. The boy and panther were made out of clay and

they were statues. They were much bigger than the two, and the boy and panther were happy.

The boy and panther had been in a good time at Rome, lots of buildings were around. The

panther went to one of the places that he knew with the boy, and it was amazing. These buildings

were so huge, about fifty feet tall. Each one was advanced for these ancient times. There were

book stores, toy stores, and lots of other stuff. The boy went to the movie theater and it was

basically like he was back at his time. The place he lives at is not Rome, but buildings keep

coming that remind him of his home. The panther decided he would stay here after he is not clay anymore, but he would still help the boy out. The boy then remembered he needed to start

working, so he went to his house. They were surprised when there was a perfectly good clay time

machine right there. The boy stepped in, and it would not work. The boy needed to figure out

how to build the perfect time machine that would take him and the panther to the future. The

panther said he wanted to be in present Rome, not ancient Rome. They are both great, but the

current Rome has more buildings and technology. The boy asked people if they are able to build

the boy and panther a time machine. None of them could, but a few said they already made one

for him. They must have been the people who came to his house. There were lots of modern day

buildings coming, there were now machines. People came to put their buildings at Rome, and the

boy found his chance to escape. The panther came with him, but the machine was protected by a

bouncy trampoline-like substance. The boy and panther tried each one, but each was protected.

The boy was upset at the panther. The panther was good, but it was his fault for trapping them.

The boy went back to his house and watched television. There were some channels about

building machines, so the boy and panther watched them. The boy was just a little upset at the

panther, not too much. He still liked the panther. The two finally found a channel where they

explained how to build the machine they needed, out of clay. The boy started working with the

panther. The machine was finished, but as always, it failed. The boy went outside to see some of

the buildings. Then someone brought the panther's mansion, which had been on sale. The

panther decided to get some money so he could buy a robot to help him. He wants to be a good

guy, so the robot would also be a good person. The panther's mansion had a time machine, so

they looked for it. There was a not from Pete, the guy he sold the mansion to. The note said that

the time machine is now owned by Pete. The panther and boy just decided to look around Rome for some time. The boy thought that these buildings were amazing, especially the oneself him

and the panther. There were lots of buildings with the boy and panther and some were just

amazing. The boy found that there was a building with lots of things that interested the boy,

because the boy told some people about him. The same thing happened for the panther. They

were not thinking about getting back to their own time, mostly about what these buildings were.

There were some airplanes and cars with a picture of the panther or the boy on it. There were

people voting for the president, and the boy and panther were some of the people they could pick

The boy went to his house and the panther went to his. Then someone came to their house and

said there was a big cave at the other side of Rome and there was a huge beast there. It was a

dragon and the person said it was made out of clay. The boy said that he needed something that

would prevent clay from growing back. The panther knew a place, so they went there. The boy

then made sure the panther would not become evil and then took what was necessary. The

panther was very powerful, so he took his clay magic with him. The panther could fly now with

his magic and his clay magic could distract the dragon and defeat it. The boy thought about if the

dragon may just be angry or something, maybe he was not evil. Then the cave they reached was

covered with unbreakable clay, so they had to use magic to break it. The dragon was just walking

around his cave. He could talk, and the boy asked if he was just angry not evil. The dragon said

that he was evil and the panther knew who he was. The panther knew, and they used to be friends

when the panther was still evil. The panther tried to tell the dragon to be good because being evil

is not fun. The good guys have always won, even if they lost. The dragon tried to think of any

other thing that would be good if he was not evil anymore. The panther kept talking to him, but then the dragon grabbed the boy and dragon and threw them out of his cave. The panther talked more to him and the dragon would not listen. The boy went to his house and there was a mini dragon there. The boy knew it must have belonged to the dragon. The small dragon was made of clay, but it was not purple, like the bigger dragon. They looked different, too. The small dragon was blue and white. The boy decided to name him Blue. Blue was not mean and liked the boy and panther. The boy asked anyone who brought the dragon, and one person said it was them. They said that they had lots of dragons and that they were giving them to everyone. They asked if the boy wanted more, but the boy wanted one dragon. The boy remembered answering someone for what his favorite colors were, and they were blue and white. The dragon jumped when the boy or panther or both came back. The dragon knew what people say, so when someone says turn the television on, he will do it. Only sometimes will he not know. The panther went to his house and there was a small green and yellow dragon there. The panther named him Green. Green could also understand what people said, but it was very rarely. He flew around the house whenever the panther came home or the boy or both of them. The two dragons knew each other, too. They have lived in the same house for a long time, so it makes sense. The dragon from the cave came out and flew around. he yelled "WHO IS BRAVE ENOUGH TO TALK TO ME. I JUST WANT TO MAKE FRIENDS!" The panther knew that when he said that it meant that he wants someone to help him be evil. The dragon breathed clay fire, which made a great decoration. The clay fire was very sticky, but edible. The boy went to the dragon and said he will be his friend. "OKAY THEN, COME TO MY CAVE ON THE OTHER SIDE OF THE PLACE THAT IS NAMED ROME NOW!" The boy went to the cave and the dragon was there. The dragon had been working with a new machine. He said the panther showed him. This would really help the boy, it was a time machine. The boy offered to test it and then return back here. The boy also brought the panther to come with him. The panther would stay at Rome and the boy would go back to his house. Then his clay phone started ringing. The butler was talking. He said that the boy's parents will be coming after a few weeks, and that the backyard had clay animals. The boy told him that he went to Rome and that there was a time machine and that he is working with someone. the butler said that the boy has been there for a few weeks, and that the boy should return. The panther said that now he will be evil, he will pretend to for some time. The dragon noticed that his eyes were green, so he was not evil. The panther said he liked green eyes better than his purple eyes. The panther could then travel with the boy. The machine then allowed the boy and panther to time travel, but then it just brought them a day further. They came back to the day before and then they told the dragon about the machine. The dragon needed to fix it, so he let the two go back to their homes. Then the pets started jumping and flying around. The pets were super hyper, so they always would be flying around or something. The boy's pet could fly a littlest the previous day, but then after he slept the dragon could fly really well. The panther's dragon could already fly really well. The panther came to the boy's house to talk about their plans with the dragon. They each thought of something that would trick the dragon into being good and then return to their own time, while letting the ancient Romans keep a dragon. The boy and panther went to the dragons cave, and they brought some clay stuff that they could make the machine out of. The machine needed to be able to travel even more. (The Innermost Cave)

The boy liked the place Rome and the stuff in it, but now he was getting bored. Now he wants to go back to his house right now, but the panther said that they needed to wait. The boy watched tv most of the time when he was bored, and the panther would, too. The panther was also getting

bored of this place. The boy tried to stay awake when the purple dragon came to get him, but it

was just too hard. The boy woke up when the dragon said that he will return the boy too his own

time and then come back. The boy would obviously stay there and not come back, so he went to

the dragon's cave. The panther came too. The panther used his magic to make sure the machine

would work. The machine had green lights and when the door opened, mist came out. The boy

was really impressed and then stepped into the machine. The boy pressed the button and the

panther came with him. Then the time machine just stayed in Rome. The boy wished that the

machine would work, so he took it and tried to fix it. Then the next morning he brought it back to

the dragons cave. The boy brought some food to the cave. Then all of a sudden, rocks fell and

covered the dragon's cave. The light of the machine was helpful, but the boy brought a bigger

light. The dragon hit his head on the side of the cave to make a hole, but it was too sealed up.

The boy brought some food, so they ate some of it. The dragon breathed the clay fire and put it

on the ground everywhere. The clay must have some sort of light. The dragon had blue eyes that

were bright and the panther knew what this meant. This meant the dragon was not evil. The boy

heard music from the dragon's clay radio. It was music from the modern times. The boy was now

trapped in a cave that was really hard to escape, and the songs help him not think about it. The

Romans were looking for the boy and panther, so they searched everywhere. Then they found the

cave of clay that was blocked by rocks. The Romans thought the panther and boy were there, so

they used different things to try and break it open. The people had broken part of it, so the people

could now have some light. The boy went to the open space and looked outside. The Romans

talked to the boy and the boy and panther also talked. The rocks were very hard to move or break, so they needed to think about what they could do. There was a machine that could be used to grab the rocks and put them to the side so the people can escape. The dragon came to talk to the Romans and they all ran away. The people were very afraid of the dragon. The panther used magic to move the rocks, but it would not work. Then the machine came, and they could only move a few rocks. The boy could squeeze himself out. The panther used magic to miniaturize himself and then went through. The boy and panther made it out, but the dragon was trapped. He was evil and there was enough room for him to escape if he squeezed through, but he stayed there. The dragon tried to grab the boy and panther but could not. The panther kept trying to tell him not to be evil, and the dragon eventually stopped being evil. The dragon stopped being evil, but now he still wanted to think about it. The boy and panther went to their house, and their dragons had grown. Now they had bigger wings. They were still kids, but they grew. The boy was very tired, so he slept. The dragon kept working. He needed to build the perfect machine for the boy to test out. The panther tried to help the dragon, he and the boy went to the stores to buy what they needed. The boy and panther never thought how much people would need to build the machine. The dragon could build machines easily, but he could not make them work. The boy helped the dragon because the boy knew about these machines. The boy and panther had finally finished helping the dragon, and the machine had the green lights. The door opened, and the mist was there again. The controls were different, they were on a touchscreen. There was also another touchscreen device that could be used to play games while you are traveling. Traveling may take some time, about ten minutes when you are traveling far into the future. The machine door closed, and the machine then transported the boy and panther to the modern day. The dragon stayed there, but then he thought about being good forever. He was now good, and now he would help the people of Rome. He went to the boy and panther's house and found the dragons. the dragon used his magic to bring them to the boy and panther. They appeared while the boy and panther were traveling. The boy then knew that the panther really is good now. The panther knew it for sure, because when the dragon says that he will be good or helpful, he will do it. The dragon has done it before, but only for a while until the panther came. The machine suddenly stopped and the boy and panther were at the time. The boy went to his house and the panther came with him. The butler already knew about the backyard, so the boy brought the panther inside. The panther liked the boy's house. The panther met the butler and then the boy's machine was outside. The panther came and noticed the clay animals. The boy brought them together and made them travel back to their own place. The panther decided that he likes to stay here. Now he is friends with the boy, so he will stay here. The pet dragons were very jumpy and when the butler saw them, he was very surprised. The butler said that the mentor had been walking by. The butler talked to the mentor, and now that the boy is back, they can talk about the new invention

The boy and panther were at the boy's mansion when they went back to Rome somehow. The machine must have not been finished. They were clay again and the dragons that were their pets came too. The dragon had still been good, but just a little evil. The boy and panther's house were still there, and the Romans had been looking for them. The boy had been very bored of this place because it is awesome and all, but not when you are there for a long time. The pet dragons had grown again, and this time they were about as tall as the table. The dragons would not grow to be very tall, they would only grow about three or four feet. The person with the dragons told them and the person had too many dragons. There were dragons owned by everyone now. The boy was

getting more bored and the panther was getting more bored. The boy wanted to go back to his

home. The panther went to his mansion, which no one had bought yet. The panther remembered

the modern times and the place that the boy and him lived in. The panther went to the dragon to

tell him about the machine, and the dragon tried to fix it. The machine was working now, and the

boy and panther went in. The dragon wanted to come too, so the machine expanded and the

dragon could travel now. The two people returned back to normal, but the dragon was still clay.

The dragon then had purple eyes and breathed the clay fire. The boy and panther figured out why

the dragon wanted to come. It was so he would be evil. The panther flew and used magic to fight

the dragon. The dragon used the clay fire, which could fight magic. There was lots of lights so it

was very hard to see. The panther accidentally moved his hand and destroyed the machine. The

panther kept fighting. The two lights were stuck at the middle, so it was hard to tell who had

been better. Then there was more purple light than the green light, so the panther was good. The

boy then saw the magic hit the dragon and the dragon fell over. The dragon was still alive, but

the magic made him very tired. The panther was weak from using the magic. The panther fell

asleep. This all happened outside the boy's house. The butler came outside to make sure the boy

was okay. Then he saw the panther and dragon and got scared. Then the boy said to the butler

how the panther was good and that he was fighting the evil dragon. The butler also said to the

boy the backyard was full of animals. The boy knew this, but he already sent them all back. The

butler said there was a panther outside. The boy explained that the panther was his pet and that

he was not dangerous to people who are not evil. He is actually very helpful and can understand

what people say. The butler also said there were two small dragons. The boy explained how those were his pet and the panther's pet. The panther ran out of the mansion to see the boy. The panther was followed by the dragons. The dragons were very happy, even the green dragon because the panther was just tired, and he knew that. The boy had not noticed the panther in a while, and the panther and dragon had become good friends. The panther went to the dragon and then lifted his paw and purple magic came out. Then the boy's friends came to see the boy. They noticed the panther and dragon, and the boy explained it to them. The dragon opened his eyes, and this time they were green. The dragon apologized and then helped the panther wake up. The panther knew that the boy was happy, and now he was happy. In a way, the panther had really been a mentor to the boy. The other mentor was also helpful, so the boy had two mentors. The mentor then came to talk to the boy about creating toys based on the animals and stuff. The mentor then got scared of the panther and dragon, but they both explained who they were and that they were good. The mentor had some examples of toy animals with him, and he showed them to the boy. The boy and everyone was really impressed, so the mentor decided to start making them. The boy went back to his house and the panther came along. The dragon just worked on the machine so he could return to Rome. The dragon had been making the green lights come, which distracted the boy and the butler. The panther was used to the lights because the panther had been working with the dragon a few years ago. The boy then knew his dragon was growing quickly. The dragon was almost as tall as the boy. The boy and panther had finally returned to their modern times, so everyone was happy. The dragon finished the machine the next day, and then he went back to Rome. He was now permanently good, because now he knew being evil is not very fun. The boy then noticed that there was something outside. There was a big tiger. The tiger had somehow entered the mansion and the panther tried to make him leave. They were fighting. The boy then noticed that the dragons had been breathing clay fire, to make it look like fire to scare off the tiger. The tiger in fact was scared, but like the panther, he was a humanoid. The tiger also had magic, and his was green. The tiger came in the house and the tiger and panther fought with magic. The panther was more experienced with magic, but the tiger had also been using magic for almost as long as the panther. The boy asked the panther what to do, and the tiger ran home.

The tiger came back to say about the big dragon the next day. The purple dragon was one of the workers and there were many more. The tiger attacked because the panther used to work for the purple dragon, but the green eyes proved that now he was not evil. The tiger was very powerful and could make portals that help you travel. The tiger created the portal that would allow them to see what the dragon had been doing. The purple dragon had been at the dragon's lair. The dragon was so enormous that he made the dragon look bug size. The dragon would be angry at the dragon after what the dragon heard, but instead he just made the dragon leave. The dragon came back to try to fight the dragon, but the dragon used magic to throw him out. The purple dragon went to his cave so he could build armor and be stronger. The dragon had some armor that would protect him. The tiger then closed the portal and then he said that they needed to prepare before fighting the dragon. The pet dragons wore armor from the boy and panther. The panther gave them magic to use when they fight. For a dragon that would make the kid look like a pebble, the boy needed to have some preparations. The panther let him use magic only when there was a fight against an evil person. The tiger went through machines to get some materials. They needed to create a big T rex robot that would be bigger than the dragon. The dinosaur needed to be very powereful, so the panther and tiger gave it magic. They started working, and by the end of the month, they would be finished with the leg. This would take many months, but it was useful, meanwhile, the boy created smaller machines to help distract the dragon. The panther gave these machines magic. The machines went through a portal the tiger created. They went to the dragons lair and were like the size of pebbles compared to the dragon. They were as tall as the boy. The panther and tiger kept working, and sometimes the boy helped build it right with his smartness. The purple dragon came from a portal he created, and he said that the dragon knew what was happening, and that he was waiting for the T rex to come. The dragon stayed and helped them. A few months passed, and the they were only done with the two legs and they connected them. The T rex was already bigger than the house, so they had to build it outside. The boy was starting to get bored, and the butler tried to cheer him up. The boy wished to have a normal life. He would rather have a normal life than be bored during the adventure. He would not be bored if he were using the T rex or something, but they would be done in like four more months. Finally four months passed, and the T ex was finished. They named it the R Tron. The big T rex could breathe purple fire. They had not yet decided to put a color on yet. They said the boy was supposed to use it but that he had to be very careful. The boy went in the robot and went through the tiger's portal. The boy arrived during the ancient Rome. The boy went to the dragons cave and then fought him. The dragon then had flaming eyes. His wings were flaming purple, and then his mouth was full of fire. The R Tron had fire eyes, and flaming teeth. It used green fire. The dragon had too much power. ''THE R TRON IS FINALLY HERE!'' is what the dragon said. The boy replied by trying to make the dragon be the good guy, because the bad guy always loses. The dragon grabbed the R Tron and made it fall over. Then he slid it out of his cave. The R Tron got back up and the dragon tried to come out, but his magic stopped him. The dragon was too powerful, he could not escape the cave. The dragon then had normal eyes and had less angry

eyes. The dragon went back to his cave. The boy got up and created the portal that would let him

come back. The people asked if he was okay and if the dragon was destroyed, but the dragon was

still there and he was still evil. They then started working. The boy helped decide the color, but it

was hard. No one agreed on one color. Some white, some green, some blue, some turquoise. The

boy was bored and just sat at his house. The boy still wished that his life was normal. He always

thought magic was awesome, but it is a little boring and old. The boy just went to his room,

where he suddenly forgot about the dragon when he started playing the new video game that

would help you create anything. The boy then could let people live in the town or village. The

panther came in to see what the boy was doing, then he started remembering the magic and stuff.

The panther knew that the boy was not interested in this adventure, but the panther said that after

this battle is over, everything will be back to normal. The boy then started felling better. The boy

came outside to see what they were doing. They were still trying to decide what colors to use.

The boy suggested black, so that the dragon could not see it. Everyone actually agreed on it and

then started painting it black. They had to paint for about four days till it was complete. The boy

helped them work on making the robot better. They gave it more magic. They made it

indestructible. The boy helped add some fiery upgrades. But the fire needed to be black so that

the dragon would not be able to see it. The tiger kept getting supplies, and the boy used his

smartness to make the robot even more powerful. They made it bigger. They gave it armor. They

made it so amazing. They knew the R Tron would take about a year to finish, but it would be

very awesome. The R Tron had also been able to clone itself so it could get more support. It

could also make fake copies to trick the dragon if it could see in the darkness. The butler had been giving snacks to help give them energy. The tiger also brought food from the places. The robot was very powerful already, and now it could be able to fly and turn into anything that will help it in battle. The boy decided to take a break and went to his friends and then he went to Tech Academy. He knew most of the classes that he missed, so he was prepared. Right now they were learning how to build their big robot. The boy needed to stay to get some information. Maybe there was something that they forgot that the boy now knows. The boy stayed for four hours and now he had so much information. He went to the tiger and then informed them about what they can do to make it stronger. The R Tron would be nice to good people, and mean to evil people. The dragon would get super angry when he sees an evil person that will not turn good. The R Tron was supposed to scare enemies to become good, and if that would not work, the R Tron would attack till the bad guy gives up. The boy had so much information. The robot was already so big and so armored up, they decided to take a break for some time. They all took the robot to a very safe place where no one will find it. They all stayed with the boy, and the dragon stayed outside with the armored pet dragons. The purple dragon then created some armor for himself and the others if they needed to fight the dragon themselves. They had been working for months, with breaks for eating and sleeping. If someone had slept, someone had to stay awake to work on the big R Tron. They woke up then took another day off. They had been working for so long, they decided to take a four day break. There were still four more long days, and the boy tried to do fun stuff so that he would be less bored after these four days of having the break. The tiger and panther were playing video games with the boy. The boy had so much fun, that he again forgot about the dragon and the magic. The tiger and panther actually smiled. They played lots of video games. The dragons outside would play outdoor games like sports and tag. The boy sometimes played with the dragons, too. Then they all got back to work when it was the fourth day. They had to finish this early, and they wanted to finish early because then they could have more breaks, especially after the dragon. The boy would not get bored, in fact, it was sort of fun to build this giant robot. The robot was very nice to the boy. The robot knew when people are not evil. If a person thinks they are evil, the dragon knows and sometimes they are not evil, just upset at something. The R Tron thought about the dragon, and the dragon was evil. The boy kept bringing materials from the stores after buying them with the mentor. The mentor then got in on the action and started to help building the machine. The mentor was very smart like the boy, and he brought some music to help them work. The music could make it fun. It was already fun, so it could be more fun. The R Tron would never be evil, only good. The R Tron also enjoyed the music. The R Tron took a while to dry from the paint, but when he did, the job was much easier. The boy looked for other people he knew to help him, like the friends of his. The boy's friends were happy to join, so they came with some of their stuff that they had been saving to build some kind of a robot. The boy's friends were also very smart, and they sometimes noticed stuff before the boy. They also could help build the machine faster. They had build many toy robots, and they had some parts left. They said that Tech Academy continued their lessons on the machine, so that might be why they were better than the boy. The boy only used what he knew and what he had heard the other day at Tech Academy. The boy helped get materials with the tiger, too. The dragons had also tried to help, because it looked really fun to work on the big robot. The boy's friends were amazed when they found out that the boy and panther owned their very own pet dragons. The boy's friends went back to ancient Rome to get some of their own pet dragons.

They came back very shortly, and they dropped the dragons off after a few hours of playing with them. The boy's friends also had more things to help them out with the huge machine right there.

The R tron had big arms and not little ones like the real T rex. The boy wanted to use the R Tron to make the bad guys become good guys. the boy knew it would take forever, but with his friends help, he could do it. They had almost been finished. There were portals that were created and the dragon sent some dragons to stop the R Tron. The dragons were fought by the purple dragon and the pet dragons, so the people could build the R Tron. The R Tron grabbed the dragons and threw them threw the portal. The people finally finished the R Tron and the panther wanted to go with the boy because the controls were created by him. The boy and panther went in, and the tiger created the portal to take them to the Dragon's cave. The portal would stay open, but the dragon closed it. The R Tron was now stuck there to fight. The purple dragon's time machine was around here, so they could escape from that. The dragon fought the R Tron and the R Tron had more power because the panther knew where the most powerful controls were. The boy had to control the arms and legs. The R Tron tried to make the dragon become a good guy. The R Tron kept trying to talk to the dragon but the dragon ignored him. The fight was very big, and there were lots of broken parts of the cave. The dragon was still more powerful. It opened the portal back to their house when the R Tron ran towards it. The R Tron appeared where the panther's house was, and before they arrived, they made sure the R Tron was just standing there. The people came over to ask about the dragon, and the dragon was still there. The boy got out and went to his house. He went to his room and played his video game. The panther knew why the boy ran to his house and his room. The boy was getting tired of this fight. The boy was getting sick of always losing. He thought the dragon was too hard to fight. It was, and the boy needed to figure out how to beat it. The boy was very smart, so he knew who to ask. He went to the museum and found the mentor there. The mentor knew about the big dragon and he tried to help the boy out with what he knew. The mentor knew so much like the boy but the mentor was smarter. The boy took notes and then went to tell the others. They were also sick of losing and were very bored of building the R Tron. The mentor knew everything that you could put on this R Tron, and everything was put on. The only thing to to is figure out the dragons weakness. The dragon's weakness was water, because the mentor could tell why the cave was so dry. The mentor knew the way to beat the dragon. There needed to be a clone of the R Tron to distract it, then the real R Tron will grab it and throw it in the water. The mentor had the machine that would clone an object. The tiger volunteered to go with the clone, and the purple dragon came with him. The boy still wanted to play video games for a while, so they stored the R Tron in the safe place. Lenny was happy when he played video games, because they were fun and Lenny forgot about the dragon. Lenny was very nice, so even if he had one controller, he would share with whoever asked him to play next. The tiger liked the video games too. The panther was very good and could help the boy with some of the levels. The rest of the people played their own video games. Lenny's friends came over to play with him, and they brought their own controllers and video games. Lenny spent more time with his friends, playing lots of video games. The panther and tiger went to the tiger's house to also play video games. They liked video games as much as the boy and his friends. The boy and his friends were playing video games and then the boy realized they had been playing for thirty minutes so they decided to do something else that was on the computer. There were lots of good games on the computer, and they showed each other some games. The dragon sent some dragons, so they fought them with the dragons. If more came, the pet dragons and purple dragons would fight them to help Lenny and the other people

Then something came from the portal the dragon made. There was a ginormous t rex and it ran after the people. They had to run and the boy jumped into the clone of the r ton and then he fought the big t rex. The t rex was very powerful because of the dragon and it was hard to fight. The r tron used fire and the t rex would just absorb its power. The t rex could talk to the boy and it tried to tell the boy to join the dragon. The boy just trapped the t rex but then it escaped. All of the people ran away. The t rex knew they were running, so it chased them. The t rex knew the mentor could help him because of his knowledge. The mentor knew what the t rex was thinking so he tried to seem dumb to the t rex. The t rex could tell if someone was smart or not. The mentor said his name was Johnny, even though it was Ron. Ron tricked the t rex and then it just stopped. The dragon still knew Ron was very smart, so the t rex got the message from the metal helmet saying that Ron was still very smart. Then Lenny came with the R Tron and fought the t rex. The t rex also wanted Lenny's knowledge,so the t rex broke the window of the r ton and grabbed the boy. The t rex started questioning him. The mentor then distracted it. The t rex ran after the mentor holding the boy. The boy needed to escape, and then suddenly lasers came out of his eyes and the t rex dropped the boy. The boy was confused, then he remembered the panther giving him magic when he really needed it. The boy could use magic to fight the big t rex. The t rex fought back. The t rex also had magic. They fought, and the panther and tiger fought it too. They blasted the helmet off. The t rex still had lots of robotic armor and it was still very powerful. The dragon then sent some dragons to help out the big t rex. The battle was very hard, so they only had to trap it to fight it later. They trapped it in a cage that was not breakable and then they put the cage where they would never escape. The place had too much magic, and it was too hard to escape. The t rex then made clones of himself. They fought the boy and the others. The battle was so hard, and this was just one of the dragons workers. The t rex was just too powerful. They kept coming. The boy had the power to fly very fast, so he took the r trons and then put them in the safe place so that no one will steal them. There were lots of minions, and the boy fought them. They trapped the t rex clones and they disappeared because they were just clones. It was like they just fought all of the evil, but there was still the dragon. Then some t rex came out of the portal wearing armor. They would protect the boy and the others, so they were very powerful. They fought the big dragon a few times, but it was too hard. The evil t rex were just the protectors that the dragon made bad guys. The boy went to the r ton and walked around with it. Then there was a ginormous snake that came out of the portal. The snake was wearing the robotic armor like the t rex, so it was the bad guy. They fought the snake. They tried to make the snake the good guy, and the snake just fought. The snake released the others from the magic cage, and they fought with the big snake. The big snake made clones of himself, and they fought and were very powerful. They fought, and the fight took forever. They finally trapped them all but by then it was already dark. They still had the final battle to prepare for, and with these battles it was very hard. They tried to avoid the enemies by disguising themselves, but it was too hard. They kept coming. They kept coming to fight the boy and the others. The dragon then talked to the boy in his mind, saying that it was too hard to fight the dragon. The dragon was too powerful with all of his magic and his powers. The dragon just wants people to help him with changing the world with his magic. The boy knew it was a trick, and then he knew he needed to prepare for the big battle. The big dragon had been trapped with his magic because the dragon was too powerful there. The dragon was trapped by his own magic, this means that he is very dangerous and that the boy has to fight him even if it will take forever and the battles with the minions just train him. The boy knew that he needed to keep fighting the monsters. The monsters would keep coming, so it was not a problem. The boy kept fighting, and then the boy knew would be ready to fight the dragon. They kept fighting them, and then the dragon appeared as a magic image. The dragon talked to the boy and he said that the monsters are staying at the dragons lair. The dragon said that he knew this would be training the boy, so the boy had to train on his own. The dragon then used magic to make the boy just relax. The boy tried to train, but now he became lazy by magic. The big dragon now could also relax, because the dragon wanted to, and the boy just wanted to train. The boy could not resist playing video games, and then he was distracted. The panther tried to make the boy ready for training. The boy was just too distracted by the magic that the dragon used on him. The boy knew that he had to get back to training, so he used his own magic to make him normal again and then he was ready for the training. The boy knew he was ready for fighting. The boy, Lenny, needed little training because the boy would be in the r ton unless it broke and then the boy had to fight using his magic. The boy knew the dragon was too powerful, and the dragon could have been training to become more powerful like the boy. The mentor had magic powers too, and he used magic to trap the dragon. The boy went into the r ton with the panther, then the mentor used magic to allow the r tron to clone itself to use to fight. The r ton was now ready, and the tiger and purple dragon took the r ton and then they had to travel to the dragon lair. They arrived there and the dragon then was trapped with magic. The r trans attacked it while it was vulnerable, then the dragon made the r

tron return to the place where the boy lived, and then they tried to get to the dragon after that

The boy was just walking to his house when a portal appeared and the boy was trapped in Rome.

The boy was trapped by some of the dragon's workers so that Lenny would not fight the dragon

and win against him. The dragon was more powerful, but the dragon knew the boy would

eventually win because the boy is the good guy. The dragon also remembered that the boy could

use magic whenever he needed it. The boy tried to escape, but it was not possible. The boy was

trapped in his own Roman house that was guarded and the windows were open but they were big

and had little lines so the boy was stuck. The boy jus watched television and then said to the

guards that the boy had given up and that he would not fight the dragon. The guards almost

thought that he was telling the truth, but then they remembered that the dragon said the boy

would try to trick them. The guard could tell the boy was lying, so they kept guarding him. The

boy needed to figure out how to get out of this place and then fight the dragon, because the

dragon was very vil and he needed to be stopped before he escapes from his magic that trapped

him. The dragon was too powerful and the boy had to trick the guards somehow. The boy then

created something out of paper that looked like him, and then the boy disguised himself as a

dragon worker, but the workers knew. They still guarded him. The boy used magic to try to

escape and then he returned to his own place. There were some dragon workers, and then the boy

went in the r ton and fought them. When the boy came, they all went back to the dragon lair. The

boy then tried to get into the dragon lair but the dragon guarded it. The dragon had just proved

that he was scared, and the boy laughed to make the dragon fight him. The dragon had said that he was scared, because if the boy fought him, the dragon could not rule a place. The dragon always wanted to rule a place, and the boy could fight him and the dragon could rule a place if the dragon won and then the boy just gave up. The boy would never give up. The boy wants to fight the dragon and make sure he will not rule a place. The dragon made the boy stay at his house and the boy played video games. The panther asked why he was playing video games, and it was to trick the dragon into letting him in to fight him. The dragon thought video games distract the boy and the boy would forget training. This was sort of true, but the boy always remembers stuff as long as something is there to remind him. The r tron which was now the t bot would reming him about the big fight with the dragon. The dragon spoke to the t bot, which could talk with the response system. The dragon tried to make the t bot a bad guy, but the t bot tried to make the dragon a good guy. The dragon then spoke to the kid and tried to trick him into becoming the bad guy, but the boy would never be the bad guy. The boy tried to tell the dragon to be a good guy and if the dragon would rule a place well, the boy would leave the dragon alone. The dragon is evil, and the dragon will never be a bad guy because it needed to rule a place and the dragon thought he needed to be a bad guy. The boy tried to explain how it is possible to be a good guy and still rule the place, but the dragon ignored it. The boy went to his mansion and when he woke up the next morning, he suddenly felt like having cheesecake so the boy looked through the fridge and then he found some cheesecake. The boy ate it when the panther came over to talk to him about how they fight the dragon. The dragon was very powerful so the dragon would be hard to fight. They thought about it and then they knew they had to use camouflage to distract the dragon then throw him in water. If the dragon touches water, then the dragon will become bones. They had to somehow get the dragon to go in the water but it's hard to get the dragon in water. The dragon is powerful and could get back to his cave. If the dragon came out of his cave it is dangerous. The dragon could have too much magic and could rule the place being the bad guy. They either had to throw him in water or make him a good guy. The t bot could trick it somehow by making the dragon scared by it. The t bot could also use the laser eyes to make the dragon a good guy because the lasers make bad guys good guys. The boy and panther needed to figure out what to to, or they could fight the dragon and then know which one to choose. They had to choose one. If the dragon became good, then the good guys would have the big dragon to protect them from anyone who is evil. The big dragon is very smart and could figure out if someone is tricking them. They had to make the dragon good to help out the people and then he could rule a place by being good to them. The boy and panther made some adjustments so that the t bots could be invisible, if the camouflage is better for other dragons because this dragon was smart. The two t bots cloned themselves when they needed to make fighting the dragon easier. They started with that move, and the dragon was trapped by all of the t bots there. The boy even had the machine that would allow him to have cheesecake whenever he wants some for himself. The panther also took some. Whenever they were tired, they could just eat this cheesecake. They all liked the cheesecake and it allowed them to have more focus

The battle had begun, and the boy started to eat cheesecake. The boy and panther sad the tiger and dragon went into their t bot and the portal to the dragon let them in. The could now fight the dragon and then save the city. There were changes like the monsters taking over where the boy lived and there were more monsters at the big cave. The big cave was probably the biggest thing the boy had known. The dragon was guarded by the snake with armor and the t rex with armor and they fought the boy so he would not fight the dragon. The boy knew he was powerful, but he

was so powerful, if the dragon made the panther or any of his friends weak, the boy would get

lots of magic and would become the king of magic. This is why the dragon had so many guards

so then he realized the boy would get more powerful, so he let the boy fight him. The dragon

fought the t bot first, and the t bot would not even have a dent. The t bot was built very well and

the panther knew how to control it. The camouflage worked because the dragon shadow would

allow them to be camoflauged. The dragon tried to throw the t bots out of his cave, but the t bots

tied him up and then created clones so they could surround it then be the heroes. They tried to

charge at the dragon, then the dragon's workers came and fought the t bots. The boy tried to get

past them and fight the dragon. The t bot is slightly bigger than the dragon, so it made it easier to

fight the dragon workers. The dragon is just too powerful. He used magic to make the t bots on

his side, so then they attacked the boy. The boy could not move around because the t bots were

fighting him. Then the boy got angry and used magic. It broke the glass and the t bots and hit the

dragon in the head. The dragon punched the t bot and it was weakened so the dragon used its fire

on it. The t bot was able to stand the fire and then the t bot launched the cheesecakes at its face.

The dragon licked it off his face but some was on his eye, then they grabbed it and dragged it

outside. The dragon opened his eyes and got the cheesecake off and then fought the t bots.

''YOU ARE MUCH BETTER THAN I KNEW, LENNY'' said the dragon. Lenny knew he said

his name to the dragon, so that it how he knows. The dragon was weak after being at the dark for

so long and seeing the sun. The dragon could barely fight. The dragon was very tired, so it fell

over and slept. They knew the dragon would eventually wake up and adapt to the sun, so they

tried to throw it in the water. The big dragon woke up and then the robot used magic to get cyborg armor. The cyborg armor is very powerful, and his attacks were more effective and the armor protected him from the sun. The dragon then went back to his cave and then tied up the two t bots. They tried to make clones and move around, but it was too hard. They tried to throw cheesecakes, and they threw them. The t bot also threw sticky stuff and made the dragon be trapped. The dragon was angry and licked the cheesecake off his face. The dragon's eyes were bursting with flames and the dragon attacked with its super long claws. They scratched the t bot because the t bot was not built to stand scratches. They fought the dragon, then the t bot had more scratches and then it broke down. The four used magic to fight the dragon. They fought and then the dragon used fire and weakened the tiger. Then the dragon and then it almost hit the panther, but the boy created the shield around them. They fought with more magic. The dragon was then scared. Lenny was already getting the green eyes from the magic. The dragon was scared and then its attacks stopped. The dragon knew it could handle the boy, after seeing the size of him. Then he knew the boy had very powerful magic from the panther, but he believed what he had known. He weakened the panther by throwing fire through the shield and then the boy got super angry. His eyes were on fire and he looked very powerful. He had orange magic, and he used the power beam against the dragon. The power beam was too powerful and the dragon was stuck and was being weakened. The boys friends were too weak to fight with him and they were next to the t bots. The boy fought with the power beam for a long time and then the dragon was dizzy and powerless. The dragon was still stuck with the sticky stuff. The boy lifted the dragon with the magic and then brought him outside. The boy threw the dragon into the water, where the dragon became a pile of bones which had sunk to the bottom of the very large ocean. The boy's friends were suddenly cured and the boy was a little weak after being so powerful. The boy was the hero with the others, but the boy had saved them all. The boy went back to his house and the animals that worked for the dragon all shrunk and were regular animals, or if it was something like the t rex they would just go to the forest or their home. The boy had been awarded with the medal by the president, because if the dragon ruled even one place, the whole world would be in danger. The boy felt so happy, and then he noticed his parents at the place the boy got his medal. The boy's parents came back from South America, and the boy was even happier now. The boy's parents were very proud of him, so was the butler. The panther had lived with the boy in his own house, and the tiger also lived separately. The boy's parents asked about the dragons, and they were fine with the idea of having the dragons as pets. The dragons were also very happy and proud of the boy. The purple dragon lived with the boy and the boy's pet dragon was pretty much an adult now. The dragons could take their armor off because the boy had saved them all. The boy played video games with his friends to celebrate. The boy also got a million dollars so he bought tons of video games and other stuff. The boy was one of the smartest people in the world, and he just saved the world. The boy had those two things to be proud about. The boy got gifts from lots of people including his parents, who bought him the new robot toy. The boy was happy about all the gifts and medals and money and saving the world from the evil dragon. The dragon could swim around in the water after it became the good guy. The dragon had been in the water when it was alive and then it came to the surface and lived in its cave. The dragon was now the good guy. The dragon always wanted to be the good guy, but his evil side made him evil. The dragon showed up through a portal to give the boy a gift of tons of video games and thanked him for helping the dragon become a better person. The boy used the scanner from the t bot he took to make sure, and the dragon really was the good guy now so the boy gave him some cheesecake. The boy also celebrated by going to his favorite restaurant and eating pizza. The boy invited his friends with him. The boy then went home and the surprises kept coming the boy kept getting gifts and money for gifts and got free passes for the movies at anytime. The boy even got some food that is just so delicious and hard to find. The good is also healthy. The boy was now known by so many people and for that the boy is happy just like he was for saving the world and getting the gifts from all of the people at his big city

www.ingramcontent.com/pod-product-compliance
Lightning Source LLC
Chambersburg PA
CBHW052020280526
45793CB00005B/1063

* 9 7 8 1 5 0 5 3 5 4 4 5 4 *